THE GARDEN OF
SHADOW &
DELIGHT

REBECCA HUBBARD

INDEPENDENT INNOVATIVE INTERNATIONAL

Published by Cinnamon Press
Meirion House,
Glan yr afon,
Tanygrisiau
Blaenau Ffestiniog,
Gwynedd, LL41 3SU
www.cinnamonpress.com
The right of Rebecca Hubbard to be identified as author of this work has been asserted by her in accordance with the Copyright, Designs and Patent Act, 1988. Copyright © 2014 Rebecca Hubbard
ISBN: 978-1-909077-37-9
British Library Cataloguing in Publication Data. A CIP record for this book can be obtained from the British Library.
Designed and typeset in Palatino by Cinnamon Press
Cover from original artwork 'Plum Tree Blossom' by Levgeniia Makhovetska, © agency Dreamstime.com
Cover design by Jan Fortune
Printed in Poland
Cinnamon Press is represented in the UK by Inpress Ltd www.inpressbooks.co.uk and in Wales by the Welsh Books Council www.cllc.org.uk

Acknowledgments

Some of these poems have previously appeared in *Acumen*, *Smiths Knoll*, *Poetry Nottingham*, *Weyfarers*, *Pennine Platform* and *Writing Women*.

Contents

Entering the Garden   5
Garden Art   7
Garden Rhythms   21
Physic Garden   35
Garden Views   47
Garden of Remembrance   61
Leaving the Garden   73

Entering the Garden

He strung the leaf door from a low bough at the end of the garden so that he could see it from the kitchen sink. In a strong wind it swung and flapped like a rag-rug hung out to dry. In the breeze it fluttered and rattled like a mass of insect wings. He'd made the door from sycamore gathered from the grass and pinned together with thorns. The brown leaves were opaque but the amber and gold ones were translucent. When lit by the sun it became a door of fire.

As he rinsed the dishes, he liked to imagine escaping through the door to a maze of gardens that lay beyond, a garden of gardens where he could sample every conceivable kind of plant, weather, scent and feeling, a paradise that allowed him to constantly travel, passing freely through time and place, and the bodies of people. What troubled him was that wherever he hung the door it cast a shadow.

Garden Art

I

Blue – what do you mean blue? Delphinium? Bluebell,
fresh or sun-faded? Flax? Speedwell? Forget-me-not?
The airy blue of love-in-the-mist or the startled blue star
of the borage flower? Late lavender grey-blue? Or do
you mean that true blue of a cornflower?

II

She sat all morning by the purple iris admiring the
petals, long tongues that lolled down from the flower's
centre where mauve intensified towards black. Leaning
over she put her eyes close up. The petal resembled
tremulous crepe blotched and patterned with
reticulated veins. Like ageing skin - she wondered if it
might be warm to the touch.
The petal quivered in the breeze, and its flickering
movement led her eye in, luring her like a bee toward
the mysterious interior of the flower. She settled back in
her chair and let her eyes readjust – once again she
could distinguish a clump of iris, the flowerbed and the
red brick wall behind. Then, taking a deep breath, she
bent forwards once more, plunging into the world of
iris. A magnified section of petal swallowed her up,
filling the whole round of her vision; the flower and the
garden lost. This was the view she wanted to paint.

III

He placed plastic figurines in the garden, positioning
miniature humans amongst flowers and weeds. Then he
took photographs – a woman sunbathing, stretched flat
on her back across the head of a sunflower. Another of a
man reading in the shade of a poppy parasol.

He was following artistic tradition. He'd seen old paintings with people sheltering like manikins under the folds of the Madonna's cloak. He too forsook scale and proportion to question humanity's place in the order of things.

IV

We search the lawn for daisies, gathering those with the fattest stems. We sit together cross-legged in the lilac's shade and, one by one, make slits in the stalks with our thumbnails. We hold up a flower and coax its stalk through another, squinting like mother threading a needle. The hairs bend as stem slips through stem, adding to the chain. As shadows lengthen we wind double garlands round our necks, daisy bracelets on each wrist and go in for tea, one thumbnail rimmed with green.

V

In the kitchen garden one leek had been left by the gardener to flower and go to seed. The stem had thickened and, though three feet tall, formed a stiff support for an elegant elongated flower bud. It resembled a stylised Russian dome stretched by its tip to breaking point. Lower down paired leaves stood out from the stalk, each folded back on itself like a bent wing. A fantastic green bird rising up on a lake in courtship.

VI

'I would like you to step outside into the garden and meet a friend,' said the old painter, Mr Wang. The student gazed at the plum tree, blossom breaking from the buds. 'This is one of the four gentlemen. He will be your first teacher.'

VII

Dry garden, no water, just combed stones and a few precipitous rocks. Within the white temple walls the mineral reigns – only patches of lichen grow on the boulders. Stand here on the raised wooden walkway and view this map of the world within.
You thirst for a place as dry as this; an oasis of rock, parched yet beautiful, a mirror of your deprivation. Here the gardener performs his duty. The arcs drawn by his rake lead you, stroke by stroke, to a place of loss and asking.

VIII

Two lengths of coat-hanger wire swivelled and twitched in his hands. The soles of his feet tingled – even through boots he could feel the subterranean waterways that coursed under the garden. He walked past magnificent specimens of beech, birch and oak, but he didn't see woods or trees, only fountains. Hundreds of gallons of dazzling water jetted upwards, thrust twenty, thirty feet into the air before breaking into plumes. Silver sprayed from twigs and leaves and dispersed over the garden in a crystalline haze

IX

The Duke loved a vista to include a fine lawn and insisted that great care was taken so the grass always looked smooth and unblemished. A band of women weeded daily, bent over, picking out thistles, dandelions and daisies. Two or three times a week they mowed – three men with scythes carefully keeping the blade at the same height for each sweep. All day to cut an acre. The lawn women followed behind, meticulously gathering up the cut grass. Every few days they brought out the roller, horses straining in their collars, always without shoes, their hooves covered in muffles to preserve the Duke's perfect green.

X

Offering round the plate, he explained that he grew eight or ten varieties each year, earlies and main crop. On one side of the dish, pieces of blue potato textured like crushed ice but warm, sweet and familiar in the mouth. On the other side, chunks of startling red flesh. Ancient Peruvian blues and reds, he said and tipped more spuds from the steamer, this time yellow. The three primaries set out on a palette.

XI

It was a state-of-the-art opera house – glass on two sides, the latest in acoustics – built in the manor garden for the summer season. The garden nestled in a perfect round of valley, the grass so sharp-edged and green it looked artificial. On the opening night rain beat down on the tented pavilions erected by the lake for picnic suppers. Water gushed over the lamps which had been meticulously set out along the length of the ha-ha in readiness for nightfall. The curved wall, built to keep the deer from the formal garden, receded into the distance, a wet serpent artfully rippling its skin.

Rain continued to hammer down all evening. Pipes jutting from the roof poured incessantly, pitching water onto the flagstones outside and adding an insistent drone to the sound of the orchestra. From the pit the harpsichord chimed like bells from a sunken village while the soprano, afloat in pastel chiffon, sang to her lovers beneath a white tree that sprouted centre stage. In the finale, its branches would burst into flames and bring the audience to their feet.

Every so often the enchantment of the stage garden with its ghostly tree was broken. A sudden torrent of water from the roof surged over the gutters and crashed below. The listeners turned to glance out. To one side lay the beds and clipped box hedges of the formal garden. Lights now glimmered in the cypresses, and in the distance a dark figure stole along the ha-ha to light the lanterns one by one. On the other side the wilderness pressed against the glass wall. Sodden trees and lewd shrubs leaned and sweated as if drawn to the delicate vibrations of the harpsichord.

Afterwards the audience picked their way across waterlogged lawns still mesmerised by the words of the aria – *happiness is a flower that passes* – and the plash of water on stone.

XII

Thin and tough as a salsify root that endures a Russian winter and sprouts green again. At eighty he still gardens twenty rods – double digs, earths up potatoes, turns out the compost heap. Copper bracelet on each wrist, flesh dried like pemmican and sharp-eyed – aphid, caterpillar, snail. His inheritance: a brown haze of earth etched into his thumb and a slight hump from years bent over.

XIII

Side by side in our hijabs we work the loom under the house eaves. Industrious girls since we were able, not looking out on the world but faced with a wall and a hundred wool threads. Without a pattern book we weave and are schooled. From the top beam the warp threads run, taut lines stretching down to us below, but we look neither up nor down. We watch for the heddle rod raising a shed, and then let the weft shoot through; colour rises up the carpet like water from a spring.

The pattern's unfinished – this rug's too vast and intricate for us to see. We know to keep our heads down and weave a rose, straight channels for water, the stem of a vine, just letting the carpet's weighty form grow. As the warp lines shorten we raise our plank seat another notch and up we go. Perched under the dripping roof we plant the four chambers of the garden with shady cypress and cedar. We put in tulips, peaches and apple trees. New wool on the shuttle – out flies a pigeon, a duck, storks, peacocks and then a herd of gazelle startle and leap light-foot into paradise.

XIV

On first entering the garden through the circle of the moon gate, you gasped. Didn't you know, flowers are most beautiful by moonlight?

XV

La Signora took the brick path that led to the kitchen garden, wearing her usual black dress and white apron, a trug on one arm. She moved swiftly, feet spilling over the sides of her well-worn work shoes. Six o'clock and a promising summer morning. A few select guests were expected for luncheon, then English afternoon tea to be served in the garden.

At the salad bed La Signora paused. The soft-headed English lettuce starting to elongate, about to bolt and no doubt bitter. Sorrel – possibly. The bold heads of radicchio caught her eye. A dashing colour combination of red and white, and the leaves would lend bite to complement the salmon. She eyed the radishes which burgeoned out of the earth like a row of pink buttons. Perhaps a few cut wafer-thin as a contrast to the cool slivers of cucumber in sandwiches at tea.

Then La Signora stepped off the path, calves disappearing in a welter of large, bristly leaves. She parted the foliage and peered in at a chaos of stalks and courgettes, skins delicately freckled. 'Uno, due, tre,' she counted. 'Quattro, cinque, sei...' Yes, there were enough. The Signora took the knife from her trug. The lightest of batters and a hot pan. 'Come è bello,' she murmured as she inspected the flower at the tip of the courgette. Today the guests would lunch on these – brilliant yellow flames.

XVI

This scruffy bit of the garden is my dye box. Wild colours everywhere. Dock, onion and rhubarb for yellow; St John's Wort or Lady's Bedstraw for red. And those spinach-like leaves are woad for blue. Garden wizardry – I sow and out spring rainbows.

XVII

She nudged the French doors open with an elbow and stepped out onto the dazzling lawn. She wore an old floral dressing gown and fleecy slippers and carried, stretched between two hands, a sheet of paper wet with blue paint. Her breath billowed, whitening the air, as she looked about for a spot where the ice crystals clustered thickly, sheathing each grass blade in diamante. Gingerly she laid the paper down and retreated to the kitchen.

She sipped coffee and re-stoked the wood-burner before returning outdoors for the paper. The paint had gathered and crystallised, a delicate feathering of blue pigment covered the sheet. Garden choreography. She'd captured the passing tracks of the frost.

XVIII

I put my ear to a snail shell and wait, just as they used to wait before the oracle's cave. Sometimes they just waited; it rained, night came, and no answer. All you can do is listen.

I slip down to rest at the height of the grass, into the layer of warm air trapped between stems. I hear the waves of heat exhaled by the earth, the cool breath under the pebbles. I listen for an answer; for stirred-up words, neglected stories buried in my belly. I grasp a handful of this crumbling loam, and see what sprouts there.

XVIX

His portrait showed the gardener's arms freckled by the amber dust from lilies; her breasts, two white peonies. Her nose, a daffodil trumpet; eyes, two brilliant gentian flowers. Her laughing mouth sprouted two rows of snowdrop teeth, and stems of love-lies-bleeding swung like crimson dreadlocks round her head.

She dined on nasturtium flower salad and rice stained yellow with stamens meticulously plucked from the saffron crocuses. For dessert she nibbled wafers sprinkled with lavender seeds. She rounded off with rose petals preserved in sugar frosting that melted on her tongue and left her breath perfumed with attar.

XX

In the front garden a blackbird on top of the ash tree, another on the house opposite perched on an aerial, a third on the adjoining roof by the chimney pot. Further down the cul-de-sac more garden birds singing. An evening concert in surround sound. Enchanted, we pause to listen, brooms in hand. Here are true artists, singing not for us but because they must.

XXI

He squinted up at the dim-lit canopy of leaves and frilly cobnuts to see if the trunk grew true, then grasped the slim sapling, lopped it and brought it down with a sharp tug. Knife in hand, he set the catch and cut off a length. He sat beside me on the garden bench, laid a piece of leather on his thigh and began. First he bent the stick in the dip just under his knee, persuading it to curve and form a ring for the base. I noticed one thickened wrist, the vice that steadied as he skimmed buttery strips from the sapling for binding. Next he split sticks to make the framework and a handle which he fixed with a God's Eye knot. Then the weaving, skein after skein of fresh, creamy wood fed between the upright ribs to build the body of the basket. He's the garden magician – with a wave of his knife he conjures forms from the trees.

XXII

Rubies. Emeralds. Topaz. Cherry tomatoes lined up like jewels on kitchen towels along the windowsill, most rounded though irregular, and a few heart-shaped. Each capped with a five-pointed hull, green tips curled back on themselves like starfish arms. Tomatoes set to bask and ripen in the September sun. She imagined shaping one from a gobbet of viscous gold, then

17

enamelling in vermillion. She would string tomato beads on a necklace – rubies, emeralds, topaz. The first piece for her autumn collection.

XXIII

Come, let me lead you up the garden path. Wiggle under the gardener's net, part the cool canes to find the leafy place where I dangle. Try my fruit – if you dare – for I'm tart as well as sweet. Pick me. Pull out my hull. Let me sit plump upon your index finger like a thimble. Suck my scarlet spawn; steal food from the lips of the gods. Come, let me lead you up the garden path. For tomorrow my flesh will wound, turning to pulp and soft white bloom.

XXIV

Searing oranges and yellows – he'd told the gardener to allow the nasturtiums free rein. The plants roamed out over the edging stones, stems scrabbling across the path and bursting into flower. Hot tones on red brick. He enjoyed the visual intensity but also the sense of impending chaos suggested by the nasturtiums' growth. Later on, in September, he anticipated more oranges and yellows but in mellower tones – Pyracantha berries interwoven with sallow passion fruit from the vine that climbed through the fence.

But today he hankered for something more subtle. He was too tired for intense colour. To escape the glaring light and sharp-edged shadows he wandered off towards the pond. Its wide expanse of water, shaded by mature trees, lay tucked away in the further reaches of the garden. On the dappled bank he set up his equipment: easel, stool, brushes, and paints. Once settled he sat in a kind of torpor for a long while. He gazed out over the pond at the round lily pads that lilted up and down on the surface whenever a coot swam past.

Every so often his eyes became unfocused so that lilies and water lost their distinctness, fragmenting into patches of colour and shadow. Or rather, what he saw was frenzied movement, a constant passing and thrilling of light and dark. Paint could capture forms, he thought, but not this deeper reality, the perpetual motion of colour and light. He leaned down and flipped open his box of oils, suddenly gripped by the desire to see if he could.

Garden Rhythms

I

The farmer is turning the year. Yesterday I watched him bring back the hedges, re-drawing boundaries smothered by the outburst of summer. Today he ploughs a curve, a dark restraining arm that reins in the stubble with its furtive crop of heartsease. Brown stripes wash over the wheat field while gulls and crows swarm, skimming the waves of new-turned earth. He stops at our hedge, raises the ploughshare's bright blades, and rattles away. Two thirds of the field turned in, the rest left for tomorrow.

I rake the last of the garden windfalls from the lawn. Tonight when I close the curtains and sit by the hearth, I'll listen to the chimney suck and blow, smelling again soft apples and loam. My mind will run free – out of the house, out of the garden and across the last acre of sun-bleached straw.

II

On the island in the high lake at Titicaca I saw the gardener gaze at the moon, waiting for the right moment to plant maize in the small plot beside his house. A waxing moon would help to swell the grain, he said.

One evening I watched him clear the weeds, prepare the ground. Next he made a hole, ramming the handle of his hoe firmly into the earth. He eased a cloth from his trouser pocket, unfolded it. He picked out a glinting nugget and held it up for me to see. 'Gold,' he said. 'A gift for La Pachamama.' He knelt down on the earth and dropped the gold into the hole, covered it, bowed his head and prayed. Then, under the rising moon, he sowed his maize.

III

There wasn't a balcony on the third floor, but from the kitchen she looked into the crown of a monumental ash tree. She enjoyed her tree garden in winter. With the leaves gone the branches cupped a glorious, empty sphere. She could make out the fine lattice of ridges and fissures on the grey bark and see the buds, black-tipped spears that waited for May to peel back their scales. Until then she breakfasted with the tree-creeper that darted up the trunk, rooting out insects with its slender bill, and the daredevil nuthatch that climbed and then descended headlong. Goldfinches and siskins flitted in and out, and sometimes a flock of long-tailed tits passed through in an excitable flutter of pink. And once, as she poured tea, a woodpecker surprised her, knocking at the window. 'Let me in! Let me in!'

IV

Every evening for an hour they lug watering cans up and down the garden path, sloshing water on runner beans and thirsty courgettes.
The bees are also hard at it in the heat. Eight hundred workers going to and fro to the pond all day, fifty trips apiece. They carry sips of water to cool the hive and thin honey for their young.

V

The maple leaves flush red this afternoon, and above our heads fairytale apples weigh the branches. But you're engrossed, monitoring the bonfire's progress, stooping, just as father used, to turn the fire in. You admire how even damp boards are eventually consumed. You angle your head against the billowing smoke, blink at the sky through a curtain of ash.

You, my father, are the fire master, pockets lined with matches, lighters. You snuff out candles between a moist finger and thumb, pinch the tips from half-smoked cigarettes, make reluctant logs blaze with a scattering of petrol.

You shift branches toward the centre of the flames, chuck back a stick with a deft hand. Sometimes you stop, insert the garden fork and lift the entire body of the fire to let it suck in air. Then round you go once more, containing the circle, keeping the fire tight. By late afternoon, the few remaining sticks burn to carpet of ash. And still you keep watch, stick in hand, attentive and wary as a shepherd.

VI

He tweaked out the bittercress and its seed head exploded. See you next week, the weed said. The war went on.

VII

Tentacles of frost grow through the hedge that bounds the garden. I gaze out across the frozen furrows. Here ploughs cut deep and turn up souls with the warp of the soil. Sometimes I glimpse reddened hands reaching up from below. And in mid-winter, cock crow carries from farm to farm, outpost to outpost.

This is the land of my forefathers. Farmhands and labourers, they shouldered sleet and wind, humbled their backs to the sun. They weaned the wilderness, slowly and imperfectly. Soil, once dragged by glaciers, now spawns packets of Tate and Lyle and these frayed leeks in my garden plot.

Yesterday I found six moles hung by their snouts from a fence, forelegs out-held and bodies locked in crucifixion. Here, in Norfolk's outlands, eyes still turn inwards to the soil; time marked by hives of sugar beet piled like rubble at the road. Here, children are born with moons of dirt in their nails.

VIII

The old woman needed two sticks to get about and had recently lost an eye. It left a dark dip like a scrunched-up prune on one side of her face. Yet she was feisty – difficult her daughter said. She just knew what she wanted and wasn't going to give up her independence, or garden, lightly.

She loved the sun, shifting a wicker chair up the garden to catch the last, low rays of autumn. In wet weather she turned on the lamp in the kitchen and read Tolstoy with one eye, or boiled up batches of damson jam.

She'd brought the seedling back from Herefordshire and now the damson tree filled half the width of the garden. It produced an abundance of tiny black-skinned fruit, the golden flesh inside turning wine-red when cooked under crumble. She always left the stones; they were far too finicky to cut out. She bagged up damsons for the freezer and filled old plastic punnets to send round to neighbours. But somehow there were always more to rain down on the long grass or, unreachable, wave to her from the uppermost twigs.

IX

A slow breach birth, and everything starved after the long freeze. Sallow grass snatches at the young light, thrush nails the rising worm. Witch-hazel buds, shrunken heads that suddenly rattle and open their censers, scattering frenetic yellow in the air. Nascent leaves try to camouflage the bony trees while the fox scents the hungry vixen. Winter, spring; expansion follows contraction.

X

After lunch they worked at another house. Old Jack took a look round – one lawn carpeted in pink plum leaves, the courtyard purple with copper beech and the mulberry papered underneath by its own lemon-yellow leaves. Some twigs with black squiggles where a few mulberries had been missed and shrivelled. Only a month ago they'd reached in for the purple fruit. And just last week Lukas had shaken the almond. The best crop ever, though the tree had grown leaves on one side only. Old Jack remembered sipping coffee while Lukas cracked the nuts with a stone on the table. This must be what it's like to have a son, he'd thought as he chewed, and the sliver of almond kernel flooded his mouth with scented milk.

XI

Mickey, the beekeeper, comes by in his veil. Sometimes he stops to give us a pot of honey. When he unscrews the lid, the lime tree blossoms for a second time. Once he passed us in a hurry, chasing a swarm's dark shadow. But today he opens the gate slowly, shoulders bowed. He carries two buckets, each filled with glassy corpses.

XII

That hot July a mouth appeared by the lavenders, dry lipped and gradually widening. The split in the earth's crust was black and endlessly thirsty. A few cans of water only moistened it, made the opening look darker, deeper, needier. I feared it would suck everything in – buckets of water, tanks and taps – all that I had. My hands felt small.

XIII

Beyond the garden the field where a tearing wind drives the seedlings toward the horizon then whips them sideways. The soil clenches tangled roots in its hard mouth so that the young wheat flails but holds.
Before this garden the first man undertook to tame these howling acres, seized by a crazed enterprise – to gash open the blank ground, score the first stuttering furrow. Then centuries and miles of treadmill, up and down, up and down, seed broadcast with a sweep of the arm into the stony craw, asking the earth to renew the gift.
Then the wait while the granaries emptied, many months for the answer. A musty hunger, or a rush of grain and straw spun into gold.

XIV

We're undertakers again. After a bitter winter we yanked out dead sage, lavenders and four pittosporums. Now drought in spring, and we must cut down the solanum that once cascaded over the corner of the shed. We clear heaps of bone-dry branches and anxiously eye the two old apple trees. They'll not last.

No rain again, though all day we've looked for it. For weeks we've endured heat and strange leaden skies. Sometimes the air suddenly cools, a slight breeze rises and we look up, expecting the release to come. But always the rain clouds pass over.

We check the mulberry, the one planted closer to the house than was sensible. Each year we wait for its fruit to swell, monitoring the change from sharp to sweet, red to black. The berries plump until their tender skins stretch and crumble to the touch, leaking savage purple juice on hands and lips. But today we find curled leaves and desiccated fruit. We stand quiet. A tremor runs through us as if we glimpsed our future, a deeper drought.

Then we rouse ourselves and talk of how the rain must come. The tree will survive, we say, or maybe we'll have to plant another. But this August there'll be no reaching into cool green leaves for mulberries. This year we'll miss a beat in our lives.

XV

Before you munch into another Cox from the fruit bowl, what about *Apis mellifera*? You depend on him. One in three bites of your food is gifted by the dusty legs of bees. Who else is there to sniff a thousand flowers a day?

XVI

At dawn she slipped out to tie sprays of millet from the tree, prayer flags to the birds. The pear tree's maze of blackened twigs had captured a portion of winter sky, holding together dozens of frozen azure pieces. She re-tied her dressing gown and, hunched against the cold, set off through the walled garden, past the sprouts, stalks lined up like an army of pockmarked trolls. She ducked under the arched doorway and headed for the pond.

Bulrushes stood locked in a slick of ice. She crouched at the pond edge, examining the air pockets trapped under the surface like pale amoebae. She pressed on the surface watching how they came to life, stretching and morphing. She leaned until the ice squeaked and broke, letting the brackish water spill over. With burning fingers she lifted out a wide window of ice so that the birds might drink, however briefly.

Then she held the ice pane up toward the sun, and stared and stared: such astonishing clarity, clusters of small pinkish leaves captured and illuminated there. A fiery, winter rose.

XVII

Monday. We plunged our heads into the azalea bush, saw yellow, heard yellow.

Tuesday. We unplugged horsetail stems, laying the jigsaw pieces on our knees.

Wednesday. We journeyed to a purple galaxy along a foxglove's speckled tongue.

Thursday. We saw rain bulge and sparkle in the crooks of lupin leaves.

Friday. I lay observing you through a forest of bluebells.

Saturday. We bagged a trophy, a crimson antler snapped from the staghorn tree.

Sunday. You tore petals from the poppy, laid them over my eyes, and blinded me.

XVIII

The bush had fallen prostrate on the soil; so much fruit
it couldn't stand. She carefully took hold of a thorny
branch, green globes dangled along the length of it, and
started picking, stooping to pick until her back hurt.
Five large bowls from a single bush. She topped and
tailed the gooseberries in the kitchen, admiring their
fine fair hairs and tight transparent skins. Plenty to
whip into gooseberry fools and to fill the conserving
pan for jam.
The next week, not a leaf left. Just a thicket of scrawny
stems and thorns. Sawflies had descended, eaten it
clean. Like locusts.

XIX

The tree's withdrawn. All the apples that suckled like a
litter of fattening piglets among its leaves have fallen to
the orchard floor. In winter time the tree dreams more
apples; their rosy, pulsing mouths tugging for the sap.

XX

For eight miles a massive wall encircles the King's
Garden, brick and ochre mud smoothed on by
uncounted hands. Outside, the arid plain. Inside, lush
green acres. Everywhere the rush of water; liberal
sluices and watercourses moisten shady orchards,
rosebeds, arbours, cypress groves and fountains. Then
under the garden wall and out, flowing on toward the
thirsty streets of Marrakech.
The King's wealth is his water; his reservoir, a lake of
unsurpassed expanse filled and re-filled by conduits
from the distant Atlas Mountains. In this sparkling
storehouse the royal children plunge and squeal. And
favoured guests wander by the lakeside, allured by
citrus scents, glimpses of glossy dates and heavy,

downy peaches. They find themselves in paradise, transported by a heavenly breeze that blows across water and brushes cool as silk on burning skin.

XXI

By this season pleasures are rare. After weeks of plenty, tart remainders in the garden – crab apples that bite sour and bitter-blue sloes in the hedge. Whatever is left intensifies, becoming more distinct and singular.
Rose hips waver in the breeze, livid clots against a leaden sky. Unmasked, the dog rose bears thorns and hard, red fruit. Not the ebullient red of summer poppies, but a concentrated scarlet that seems to emanate from within. Each hip conceals choking fibres laced with a savage distillate brewed from September heat, the rummaging of hoverflies and the memory of a fragrance that vanished with the wind.

XXII

A surprise bouquet – a clump of pink cyclamens. Fragrant butterflies, they appeared under the bare trees, from nowhere.

XXIII

Old Jack went back for a rake and found Lukas crouched under the birches, brushing aside fallen leaves with a stubby hand. 'Mushrooms,' he said, and slid a knife from his trouser pocket. 'Better to cut, then more will come.' Lukas's phone rang – Margarita, the fiancée, again. Jack had a glimpse of her once and remembered fairytale locks hanging down to her waist.

'*Blamba!*' said Lukas. 'She says I like Laura better.' Jack shrugged. 'There's no understanding them,' he said. Thirty years with his wife, ten apart and none the wiser. 'These are top, top mushrooms,' said Lukas.

'Are they now? Well, I'm not touching them.'

Lukas sighed. 'Look, I eat them and I come to work next day. In Lithuania, we go every year to the forest. Full moon is best. Lots of people go from my city.' Everything's better in Lithuania, thought Jack. He'd heard it all – real snow, real women, real vodka. Lukas laid the mushroom in his bucket already half-filled with quinces. Nobody ate them in England. He'd take them home, to Margarita, to make things right.

The phone again. A Russian friend this time. So many friends, thought Jack. Lithuania was certainly different. 'Now I'm in trouble with her, I can't go to watch Chelsea at Misha's.' Lukas made a face. 'She's got you round her little finger,' said Jack. Nice, he thought, to have someone to give in to.

'She'll be happy when I come home early with quinces and top, top mushrooms; some for supper and some in the freezer for the twelve dishes of Christmas,' said Lukas. 'I like Laura better, she says. So tonight, no Misha, no Laura. We'll prepare mushrooms and fruit.' Jack imagined them together, cutting the fragrant quinces, making up. Lukas sang and went on searching the lawn for mushrooms. Always it was Lithuanian love songs. Jack knew he'd never been happy like that.

Physic Garden

I

A blackbird sings from the top of the great sequoia that dwarfs the mansion house, upper branches raised, the lower limbs trailing onto the lawn. The bird sings, thin toes clasped round a pale, dead twig. Its voice carries to the hollyhock spires, wet-petaled roses and gardeners below. It travels into the offices and corridors, like bubbles threading through water, and seeps down into the tree's resinous heartwood. Perched high on a wizened finger, the blackbird is singing the tree through its first small death, and into magnificent summer.

II

I see only a distant garden now, a flat picture garden framed by a window, scentless and removed. I lie indoors battling with cells that proliferate inside me like ground elder. There's no rooting that out for good. Today, to cheer me, she arrived with a bouquet in an egg cup – even they couldn't refuse me that at my bedside. Pyracantha and a sprig of piny evergreen. Real rain on the berries. How they glowed. So orange. They still burn inside me.

III

He drove me up to his place in the mountains, he'd promised to show me his garden. We sped round hairpin bends, braked for a herd of goats that stood bleating, bells clinking, until a wild boy on a moped drove them on.
In the garden an abundance of pomegranates, figs, beans and tomatoes. And up near the vines a bee hive dripping with honey.

A dusty pick-up screeched to a halt; friends to help with the harvest. Bunches of grapes as long an arm, and heavy. The warm juice ran. My hands grew sticky. I wore a fertiliser bag for an apron and stared in a daze down the gorge to the winking sea as they sang.
All day in the heat they worked: picked, swung boxes, sweated, laughed, larked like madmen. I could only make out the frenzy of names that flowed from their purple lips; Hercules, Pericles, Dionysus...

IV

The X-ray clearly showed the cuneiform bones were damaged. It was her digging foot. Crumbs and white powder. Already turning to bone meal, she noted.

V

'Turning to the glorious gates of the Physic Garden, we can see the serpent of disease, Python, and the figure of Apollo, God of medicine and fifteen other things besides. These gates only open to admit senior royals, and the annual delivery of manure.'

VI

She was given the fish, a Koi carp, not long after meeting her guru. She called it Jaws and put it in the garden pond. Not long after the dreams began. Every time a fish appeared. Seven fish in a pond or a greenish man stood on the back of a fish as it swam downstream. Years later Jaws died. In the last dream she looked into the pond. No fish. No reflection. Nothing.

She held a party. Eighteen guests. She baked a whole salmon. After eating they read aloud her eighteen fish dreams. It was her way to say goodbye to Jaws and her old shark self.

Then she began to sculpt a life-sized terracotta fish. The important part was emptying him out, putting her hand inside and scooping out the moist red clay. Handful by handful, to make space inside.

She stood Jaws at the side of the pond. It had taken most of a lifetime to clean out the guts, the anger, the losses. Now all she wanted to be was empty.

VII

He does not run anymore, but walks stiffly through the garden, past vermillion roses and ferns patterned like doilies. Head bowed over his book, he shields himself from unexpected colours and hoverflies. He lives at one remove from us now. First we noticed how his gaze glanced off. He refused our faces, and then deleted our names. Aged five, he has taken a terrible vow of silence: mute because there is something huge that cannot be laid before us. We walk the garden path in parallel, surrounded by our loss. He's a thin, fierce figure clutching a book where flowers and trees are knowable and labelled. An ascetic, he flees inward to a bone-dry place that promises integrity. And neither I nor all the flush and greenness of the garden can woo him back.

VIII

In the soft sound-world of evening, bullocks snatch and crop behind the garden hedge. We listen to their breath, huffed through damp nostrils, and fancy we hear the brush of eyelashes as they blink at flies. In our shadowy place at the pond's edge, iris stems burst from silt and a frog creaks like a leather boot. Coot chicks pipe while their mother dips and fetches. Tiny fish flip at the surface and glimpse us laughing.

When we sleep we will return here like thirsty reeds to be fed by dancing fish. All night long the pond will sit like a black eye in our garden, the bullocks grazing the fence, young reeds sprouting through the fragrant mud. And tonight green buds will pulse and push inside our secret mouths, then burst out, festooning our tongues, our ears, our eyes.

IX

Often I run from the house, sleepless and driven by terrors. I spend nights under the neon sky, an orange tablecloth above and far away. I curl on the blood-clot earth or cleave to the sycamore. Cold, wet, rough – its bark on my face is father comfort. Tree-body rocking in the wind like mother. At four in the morning, there is nothing, no one, just neon light. Hold onto the sycamore.

X

Wipe your eyes. Come and listen to the first spring shrub flowering in my garden. This currant bush grows unchecked, pushing over and under next door's fence. You mustn't mind the leaves that smell so strange. See here, the flowers that look first like raspberries, then explode and fade to palest pink - and how many! Stand here before the wall of blossom. Let yourself be comforted by the warm drone of the honeybees and the bumbles' fiery roar.

XI

At last the baby was asleep. She could slip away, escape last night's dishes stacked in the sink, the piles of dirty washing. She wandered down to the giant willow tree that almost filled the lower part of the garden. Parting its trailing branches she stepped inside, letting the leafy doorway swish closed behind her. Inside tranquil yellow light filtered into a domed room, the willow's trunk a column at its centre. A secret world, baby and dishes far away.

She lay on her back and breathed. Long breath out, counting to four. She was tired, but yoga would revive her. A few stretches and then her favourite, *Sarvangasana*, the shoulder stand. Head and neck flat on the earth, hands supporting her back, she stayed inverted and upright, breathing into the pose.

She stared up at her feet and the leafy ceiling and smiled; it was so much better this way up. Lately she'd been weighed down, as if she shouldered a massive burden. But now this weight rested on the ground, a firm base from which spine and legs rose up steadily like a plant stem from the earth. She felt light, refreshed. No wonder yogis called *Sarvangasana* the mother of all poses, she thought. It defied gravity. She was no longer earth-bound. Legs and feet reached skywards, the delicate flower of her being offering itself.

XII

The girl knelt and scooped out a hole in the flowerbed, a nestling cradled where her skirt sagged between her thighs. She had found the chick, neck outstretched, yellow-rimmed beak propped on a pebble. Its skin dotted, feathers yet to sprout, and the eyes, dark and protruding, still sealed shut. She picked up the rounded body between finger and thumb, the head flopped down, and she quickly placed it in the hole and covered it with earth.

A while later the girl ran from the house full pelt. Her mother had said something about nestlings sometimes seeming dead but being merely cold. The girl scrabbled to uncover the tiny corpse, grains of soil stuck to its clammy skin.

Cupping the nestling against her chest, she sat on the doorstep and breathed over its puckered body, willing it to move. 'Please, please,' she whispered. Another breath. Did it twitch? She exhaled again and searched for a sign. Surely it shifted. Or had she tipped her hand? Another breath. The head jerked. The beak strained upward, just a fraction, instinctively reaching for food. The girl turned to the door. 'It's alive,' she shrieked to her mother. 'Alive!'

XIII

What's happened to the lawn?
Ah...
Did it get burnt or something?
It was Freddie.
What, your lad?
Yes, we had another row, and I sent him to cool off in the garden.

XIV

It is strange that the streets in every town are quiet when in each house hearts beat with passion yet shrivel for the want of it.

Enter the midnight gardener. His barrow crushes the wayward mint as he walks the garden paths. Its fresh green fragrance creeps under the doors and into the sleepers' dreams. Catching sight of themselves in the winking mirror of his watering can, they awake.

They get up and run naked into the garden to dance with apple trees, skin flushed and ripe as fruit. In the moonlit garden poets, painters and singers revive. They rattle dried honesty pods, beat sticks on the bars of the gate, yowl like randy alley cats. How they gasp at the sudden colour in their lives. Salt and sweet tasted again.

XV

He wouldn't be any trouble, not if I know men. Something softens a man when he lives by the earth. A soldier but he'll set weapons aside for a hoe. Working the land is a physic. The garden calls in the sick, they answer like chickens to the rattle of corn in a bowl.

He'll mend by me, I'm certain. Lying in bed at night he'll hear the plants grow: ivy sprouting through the broken plaster, holly knocking at the roof tiles, roots pushing through the soil under the house – white strings that feel past the stones. Those sounds reach deep into a man. He'll stop hating and cursing and learn to find his way round.

Summer in my garden is like a high tide rising – foxgloves and cow parsley shoot skyward. That'll touch him. And in spring we'll tap the birch tree, watch fresh sap pour into the cup and drink. Green tonic heartens a man after war or winter.

But for now I watch over him. Night after night he sleeps like a vagrant under my hedge. I feel like a blackbird tending a nest. People laugh, I know, but I've found what's true. Making love under the lilac, buttercups quivering. Together we'll make the trouble pass.

XVI

From the garden this morning, sweet chestnuts, fat and
sleek. They glow, touchstones in my bag, as I head for
the city.　　Marching, head down, through tunnels,
streets, glass, metal, rivers of unmet eyes, I reach in and
take hold. A dug to latch me to earth.

XVII

Everywhere he looked emerald cushions and lime
carpets. Two hundred kinds of moss grew in the temple
garden – even the hazy sunlight was tinged a delicate
green. It played on the boy's clothes, sinking into his
body until his bones grew warm and soft. He felt weak
so, as no one was about, he laid facedown on the mossy
ground. He brushed his cheeks repeatedly against
miniature pine forests, and let his fingers caress the
velvety hummocks that rose and fell like swollen bellies
around him.
He breathed in the sweet, woody fragrance of decay
and rested. The moss shaped itself to his contours in
that longed-for caress. The boy gave himself up,
returned, complete again, yielding to the ground like a
child. In the outline of one mossy tummock, he
dreamily retraced the curve of his mother's neck. He
recalled a protruding mole that had grown there, its
surface crinkled like a cauliflower. Not ugly but a
certain landmark on a living landscape. He used to
reach out, touch it and know: here she is, and here am I.
Then, out of nowhere, a swarm of angry monks. 'Ai!
Ai!' they shouted as they set about the boy, bamboo
rods flailing. He blinked, struggled to his feet, arms
over his head to fend off the blows. 'Ai! Ai! Ai!' yelled
the monks and drove him from the garden.

All night he lay awake on bare ground outside the temple wall. The welts from the bamboo rods stung like wasps but he didn't care. Wide-eyed he gazed up at the blissful bowl of the sky; the heavens were mossy, the stars twinkled green. Even when he closed his eyes – green.

XVIII

At first she wondered why the Germans had dropped seeds as well as bombs in her garden. Swathes of rosebay willow herb sprang up overnight on rubble piles. Vibrant yellow ragwort, nettles, sorrel, dock and poppies appeared on the burned-out site of their London terrace. After flames and ruins, incredible colour. Buried seeds re-greened the city, signalling the way.

XIX

The consulting room was cool, tucked as it was under the arm of an oak that reached over the Physic Garden's wall. A woman sat bolt upright among the shelves of brown and green bottles. Through the window, she watched the tall figure of the herbalist, a giant wader-bird on thin shanks, bending and dipping among the flowerbeds. She'd found herself telling him everything. About the long labour that delivered her a tiny corpse. About pacing the house at night, the hours magnified by nightmare thoughts, thoughts that circled, attacked, that were unstoppable.

The herbalist seemed oblivious to the steady rain. When he came in, water dripped from his grey hair. He smiled as he spread paper on the table. 'These,' he said, opening the long hinge of his hand, 'are to form your core.' He placed three wheat seeds on the paper. The woman drew her chair nearer. 'And this is woundwort – some people call it clown's woundwort.'

'Clowns?' she said.

'Yes, the ones with red noses.' He slipped the woundwort under the wheat.

'Archangel,' he said holding up a leaf, 'a variegated type for silver.'

'Why silver?'

'To bring you money, and moonlight. And here's oak for strength and ivy – its new shoots will soon cling on, once they find something.' He added them to the other leaves. 'Now periwinkle, a magic plant for joining things, and three yarrow stems wound together to go round them all.'

'What for?'

'To strengthen your aura,' he replied. He laid a large leaf on his palm and held it out to the woman – it felt dry and furry. 'Motherwort, for women's problems.' He wrapped the motherwort around the other leaves then folded the paper to make a small, square packet.

'It's a big talisman,' he said. 'Time for string.' He brought red cotton. 'Talismans must always be tied with red,' he said and she put her finger so he could tie the knot. The herbalist went to the cupboard for a night light. 'Special wax,' he said as wax dripped onto the knot. 'Slow burning, of course, to last eight hours, and to ward off nightmares. Now, keep this on or about you.' The woman pushed the talisman into her skirt pocket and kept her hand there. Something to hold to when the bad thoughts came.

Garden Views

I

'Highly invasive,' explained the official in boots and reflective jacket. '*Buddleia davidii,* a Chinese immigrant adapting from lime cliffs to the mortar in brickwork. Hundreds of miles of British railways colonised. But the new magic bullet does the trick – systemic herbicide shot directly into its vascular bundle.'
On the other side of the fence, the man with the dog didn't seem to understand. Each summer hundreds of long mauve flower heads festooned the siding. They nodded constantly, mobbed by clouds of painted ladies, peacocks, green-veined whites. 'But they're our butterfly bushes,' he said.

II

Valerian flowers, bleached to sombre pink, grew among the shingle, their wasted stems leaning against a driftwood tree trunk. This was their garden, an area bounded by sea junk: leached-out posts, a couple of ropes coiled like cobras and a boat winch with broken cogs. The same self-seeded plants grew as in the rest of the stony borderland that tied land and shore together. Coarse grass, scant sorrel and a stunted mallow somehow survived salt winds and brutal sun. On the more sheltered side of the house a dog rose waved a dragon-spined whip from side to side, woody stem crusted with red and yellow lichen.
They'd made their home in a fisherman's clapboard cabin, paintwork sapped to a soft gull-grey. At dusk its elongated shadow seeped out of the garden and down the pebble slopes toward the sea. A gigantic anchor at the doorstep – rust in thick flakes and capped with two mighty arrowheads – seemed to hold the hut in place when gales hurled foam and shingle up the beach. Extremity had drawn them there. They lived better in the face of constant vulnerability; the wilderness – sea,

weather, stone – constantly trying to claim house and garden back.

III

Plentiful green apples hung among the leaves. I imagined scented pies, oat-topped crumbles, wedges of Dorset apple cake, puree sliding into gleaming jars, peel in roundels, gnawed cores, dark cloves, flaking shafts of cinnamon, cookers stuffed with butter and raisins, plagues of boozy wasps, starlings pecking at a mush of windfalls.

But he rested a large working hand on the tree and gazing up said, 'You'd get a bench from the trunk and five hundred spoons from that branch.'

IV

Even inside the shed I catch the heady perfume that the mauve phlox blasts into the warm evening air. Five miles off, a butterfly tastes it on the wind.

V

A cherry stone – a minuscule tree locked in a box.

A cherry stone – a parched place, a desert longing for moisture.

A cherry stone – a tree under restraint, in waiting for months, years, until conditions are right.

A cherry stone – a hidden treasure, flushed pink blossom against blue sky.

A cherry stone – a seeker travelling up and down, the journey's end another cherry stone.

VI

She wanted a laurel hedge, thick and high like the one
she'd once seen taller than a house. She sought privacy;
not to sunbathe topless on the lawn but to shut out
children, telephones, questions. She didn't want to hear
someone sneezing next door. She came out in the
garden to listen to what was going on within.

He suggested privet kept trimmed to a reasonable
height, a hedge that allowed him to hail the neighbours
as they hung out the washing or to gaze into the field
when the combine cut the wheat. A garden hedge was a
boundary for crossing, for the giving and receiving of
gifts – spare seeds in old envelopes, news from the
village, a clutch of courgettes.

VII

Greet your fellow gardener, the ant. Such attention and
sophistication – vents and tunnels attuned to the
delicacy of the mushroom crop, moulds zapped with
antibiotic secretions. And their landscaping – such
fairytale feats with mounds of sand and earth.

VIII

George, the gardener, has a theory; in all languages the
name for butterfly is beautiful.

Summer Bird, Living Coal, Little Flying Creature.
Butter-licker, Butter-thief, Butter-shit.
God's Little Cow, Petal Spreading Out.
Mary Alights, God's Bee, Soul Breath.

Zomerfeygele, Glöyn Byw, Etelachań.
Botterlicker, Molkendiep, Boterschijte.
Bozhia Korovka, Petalouda.
Mariposa, Seilleann-dé, Psyche.

51

IX

Aspire to the plum tree's purple generosity. Everywhere fruit, waste and wasps; bowed down with plenty, and giving carelessly.

X

As a child she'd looked in the mirror hoping to see herself but soon realised that it didn't show everything. Now an old woman, she sat in the garden and looked at a tree. She thought about its roots and the mystery, about what was hidden in darkness and funded such remarkable growth.

XI

I discovered the stone while playing under the pear tree where the blackbirds gorged on rotting fruit. I brought it to my father. A stone: slate grey and smooth, cool as an egg, tasting of soil and fermented pears, an oval shape that satisfied my palm. Picked from many scattered on the earth, chosen from the commonality of stone, this was my gift.

XII

The sheen of one pea punctured, a smattering of pinprick powder heaped on the skin beside a minute hole. Green drill dust from the pea worm. He hoops and arches across the pea's surface, a snip of embroidery thread as pea-green as his feed. I've just exploded the world where he feasted. Just a moment ago his urgent jaws ground through a line of spherical warehouses. I flick the worm and drive my thumb down the pod. Peas drum into the pan.

XIII

Ah, the new water butt. Wonder how much rain it catches. Height, say, 1.5m, diameter 75cm. Use volume = $\pi r^2 \times h$. Approximately 497.8 litres. Interesting.

What if the lawn mower broke and you had to use a goat. Rectangular lawn, 10m by 5m. Goat tethered to a post (P) at the middle of one side of the lawn on a rope 1.5m long. What area could it mow? Easy. A semicircle, area: $1.5 \times 2\pi = 9.43m^2$.

The cold frame. Do germination rates for parsley vary over the week? Out of fifty seeds planted each day how many grow? Draw a leaf and stem diagram to show results.

XIV

He didn't believe a word of her alternative mumbo-jumbo. 'The garden's a first-aid kit,' she said. 'Snap off a piece of aloe, its sap will cool your sunburnt shoulders.' But he'd felt how rue blistered skin. 'Comfrey's useful for relieving aching joints,' she insisted, 'while lavender soothes an itchy insect bite. To staunch a cut, take yarrow leaves, chew and apply.'

He knew otherwise – sickness and malevolence flourished in the garden. He always weeded carefully around the columbine. Pretty but malicious – toxins in seed and root, enough to stop your heart. When he mowed the lawn he wondered about the body count of arum lilies, foxgloves, and the laburnum tree.

He began to put warning signs in the borders. Keep Children Out. No Pets. Don't Touch. Danger of Asphyxiation, Kidney Failure, Madness. They divorced. He built a high stone wall around the garden, topped by shards of glass, and added an iron gate and railings wrought with snakes and skulls. But still fear spread like poison ivy. He incarcerated the lily-of-the-valley in a metal cage, hacked down the yew tree, stamped on the lords and ladies' luminous berries.

Even his sleep was poisoned. Each night he dreamed of a garden in Kerala hedged about with *Cerbera odollam*. These suicide trees bowed down before him, presenting a hundred starry, fragrant flowers and green fruit. Always a single seed lay cracked and smiling on the earth, its white meat slowly turning to violet and quietly, insistently, calling his name.

XV

'But it's still a perfectly good lettuce,' he said.

'I'll not be eating that,' she replied. 'It's riddled with holes.'

'What *are* you doing with the secateurs?'

'They'll scoff the lot if we let them. My father always went after them at night with a packet of Saxa.'

'Just put the slugs here, in the jam jar. I'll take them to the gasworks.'

By moonlight, beside the gas bells, the rescued slugs do body art: liquid silver trailed over dewy grass.

XVI

I stroll about the garden with old Evelyn shuffling beside on her walking frame. We pause to inspect an apple tree by the path, exclaiming at the fruit that bends the branches; some still small but other apples large and ripe, skins burnished. Evelyn reaches out a hand. 'That's stealing!' I say. 'Why shouldn't I have an apple? There's loads,' she says. She nudges me and grins in that devil-may-care way of hers. 'You can have one too,' she says. Then glancing over her shoulder, Evelyn starts stuffing apples into her handbag. 'Come on,' she says and scoots off, laughing, laughing all the way. What can I do but follow?

XVII

I lie flat, face to face, the ground a body under me,
quickening. Grass stems wave – the brush of lips. New-
turned earth smokes, releases incense, but this sun-
baked soil is hard and hot. I sip like a bee at her grainy
mouth. I want her to take all of me in, to be swallowed,
and go under, to oblivion. Under soil, under stone,
smothered by the weight of darkness, enfolded and
silenced in her jet-black depths.

XVIII

First we simply used our eyes and saw a green leaf –
veins, stalk, blade.
Then we sliced the leaf and put it under the microscope,
noting cells – walls, nuclei, grains of starch.
Now we film inside in real time, magnifying the dance
of the chloroplasts. We watch how they jostle at the
leaf's surface, hustling for the best of the light.
Later we'll witness the roar of electrons across vast and
sombre spaces.

XIX

Once upon a time three measly beans got hurled out of
a window into a garden. They'd been swapped for the
price of a cow. Overnight a beanstalk sprouted.
Whoosh! A green ladder leading to a dangerous realm
of giants, magic lyres and golden eggs. What a good
exchange: milk for growth.

XX

That nettle you're about to yank out is a 'she' not an 'it'.
Let me introduce you to *Urtica dioica* – the nettle of the
two households. Don't be shy; take a peek at her
drooping flowers. And those nettles living on the other
side of the fence are the menfolk. Look, flowers held
erect in the wind!

XXI

Sprouts and carrots from the garden. Divine lunch?
Piles of shock-orange discs and miniature cabbages on
my plate. Punch-drunk gladness – unprompted grace
striking through clouds of steam. A fine harvest. Plenty.
And I, the glorious reaper, plunging the lightning fork
into crisp, green marbles.

XXII

That morning another revelation. She awoke to a strip
of wallpaper peeled from the bedroom wall like a petal
and ablaze with blinding-white light. She shielded her
eyes and thought of the garden. Last night the
remaining berry – the one that the frenzied starlings
missed – must have dropped from the ash tree. In her
mind's eye she saw the fruit fall in a flash of searing
orange. It plummeted towards the stone where, in
summer, the children balanced to reach the lowest
branch and swing. The berry splattered on the stepping
stone. Flesh split, seed split. Then matter itself divided
and revealed God's atomic light.

XXIII

Think before you uproot that self-seeded sycamore.
Every leaf is peppered with pores like tiny green
mouths. And lips guard each mouth – they swell and it
opens, they go flaccid and it closes. This is how the
sycamore breathes. What's more, its out-breath is just
what you need – oxygen. If that's not enough to stay
your hand, then consider how this seedling made itself
– stem, bark, roots, leaf – from sunlight and you; your
old breath lives again in that sycamore.

XXIV

I swim in a suspension of gold-green silt and sunlight; a
water-snake easing my silky way across the pond.
Rushes creak. A coot calls. Past the duck dreaming on
her nest. Past the bulrushes, blasted open, seed spilling
like slow-motion spiders over the water.
Belly-up I float among the lily pads. Petals gone, they
still hold up empty stalks like periscopes. My face, disc-
like, turns towards the late summer sun. Hair spreads
and weaves. Eyelids droop.
Later my legs tremble when I return to the firmness of
the bank-side. Flesh a shocking white, thighs crisp and
cold as lotus root.

XXV

In Kent, the Garden of England, an unearthly garden.
Cabbages used to grow here in Thanet, now acres of
flashing greenhouses, pitched roofs zigzagging over the
flatlands. Inside, warmth and abundance; peppers and
cucumbers grown to perfection. A 21st-century paradise.
At Planet Thanet everything is perfect. Perfect light –
sun by day, artificial light by night. Perfect food –
balanced minerals, nutrients, extra CO_2 to pump-prime
growth. Perfect climate – vents, heaters, humidity

control. Perfect plants – stock certified, virus free. Perfect hygiene – crops suspended from ceilings in hydroponic rows, roots never touching the chalky soil below. Sterile. Managed. Perfect. No earth.

XXVI

My ears rang after the blast. I'd seen the crown of the great sequoia struck and plummet and ran out through the driving rain to see if the gardeners were hurt. 'The world went white for a second,' said one, his eyes wide and bright. 'And the noise.' The other waved elated arms in a cloud of splintered wood and dust. 'Wonderful. To witness *that*,' he said. His eyes burned electric blue and the air around him bristled.

XXVII

By the garden hedge I play, spinning Tom Thumb adventures in forests of twigs. I can do magic – make a hump of moss swim like an emerald whale through the swell of a soil sea. And with a swish of my twisted stick I too can dive in, grow breasts, plump and white, and a scaly tail to drive me through the waves. In my garden, everything is possible – I am whale and girl and mermaid, earth is an ocean and everything is always green and true.

XXVIII

'It's time we took that in hand, my lad,' said Old Jack. Over the summer months tendrils of wisteria had escaped onto the roof again. 'Good, good,' said Lukas. 'I'll get my ladder.' In June visitors greatly admired the mansion house gardens. Everyone was intoxicated by the mauve wisteria, the blooms that swung hypnotically releasing heady clouds of pollen and scent.

Years back, Jack had helped pin the unruly stems down with wire and bolts so that two neat tiers ran round the bays and along the white façade.

Jack rocked the ladder to settle its footing and rested a boot on the bottom rung. Not tall but strong, thought Jack, watching Lukas go up. He lifted manure sacks like they were sugar bags. 'Two hands on the ladder,' Jack ordered. They were working in view of the office. 'Thank you – I look forward to seeing my grandchildren,' Lukas called down. Damn Health and Safety. Out of sight, they did as they liked. Lukas chanced it on walls and trees. Jack didn't mind flouting rules as long as they kept their noses clean, and he enjoyed seeing Lukas perched on a branch, smoking and sawing, lording it over the gardens.

'God's Little Cows!' said Lukas snapping a photo with his phone. He climbed down to Jack – a ladybird colony under the windowsill, a hundred or more. 'Maybe British, maybe those bloody foreigner ones,' he said.

Later they tramped to the shed for lunch. 'Good, good,' said Lukas, pouring amber liquid into his tea. Quince juice, homemade and kept in a plastic bottle. 'The Lemon of the East it might be, but I like my tea the English way. Milk and two sugars,' said Old Jack. He watched Lukas set his teabag aside on a spoon. He would put it wrapped up in his pocket for later. Jack had to admire his frugality. This lad knew about hardship – uncles carted off to Siberia, factories closed when the Russians left, and waking before dawn to work his auntie's dacha.

XXIX

A windowless lean-to rested against the wall. The new garden boy tried the handle – locked. He needed to get in. The head gardener had just told him: 'Weeds are the gardener's enemy. Get a hoe.' He rattled the door in frustration, then sank to the ground and began to examine his feet. He'd taken off his boots because the stiff leather chafed. Now, with the exception of his arches, the soles of his feet were green. 'Barrow? Trowel? Dibber?' The garden boy looked about. A small, hunched-up man leaned out of the tool shed.

'Spade? Shovel? Ball of string?'

'A hoe,' ventured the garden boy, getting to his feet.

'And exactly what kind of a hoe would you be wanting?'

The boy shrugged his shoulders. 'Just a hoe. A common or garden hoe, I s'pose.'

'We've got the American Standard – that's an old standby,' The man disappeared into the shed. There was a clanging of metal – watering cans or buckets – and he yelled above the din: 'If you're wanting a hoe with a nose for weeds, take the Rogue Dog Hoe. Or use a Circle Hoe to run circles round them.'

The man suddenly stuck his head out. 'Fancy the Cobrahead? No weed is safe from its strike.'

He disappeared again. 'Tired of pulling? Try the Push Hoe. Or if you can't decide to push or pull, take the Scuffle. Alternatively, let the Ro Ho Hoeing Machine do the hoeing for you.'

'Any hoe will do,' the boy shouted back.

The man's head popped out momentarily. 'Gotta have the right tool for the job, lad.'

'For rough land, I've a Grub Hoe,' he called from the interior. 'That's a hardworking hoe. Then there's the Winged Weeder – a superhero of a hoe.'

He reappeared at the door. 'Is it decking you're weeding? In that case you'd be needing a Deck Digger Hoe.' He went in and continued his search. 'Stirrup Hoe, Dutch Hoe, Half Moon Hoe, Fork Hoe, Putter Hoe – not for golf though.'

Then he came out, slammed the shed door and locked it. 'Sorry lad,' he said pocketing the key and setting off down the path. 'No common or garden hoe to be had.'

Garden of Remembrance

I

The gardener told me of all the winds she knew, and their names. She'd seen the shape of the wind when the rains blew slantwise. And once she'd glimpsed a great whisk of tired souls and dust turn and lift from the garden.

II

The Administrator was weary of the Emperor's demands. He longed for a refuge from the court, so he made a garden. He began by placing tall thin rocks chosen for their texture, they gave an impression of lightness, almost transparency. The rocks were reminiscent of his beloved Yellow Mountains.
In the garden, he could imagine wandering in his homeland again as his eye followed the course of the stream meandering, dragon-like, under small bridges, disappearing behind a rock and reappearing beside a bamboo grove. A small garden pavilion took him back to days spent with a few close friends in the mountains where they would paint, recite poetry, and drink *baijui*. Sometimes his thoughts turned to the hours spent contemplating the distant peaks rising out of the mist. Such imaginings sweetened his exile.

III

That's where they buried the old dog, the gardener's gentle lurcher. He followed him from garden to garden, bed to bed, and slept on an old potato sack in the shed when it rained. Everyone who encountered the gardener coming up the path with a barrow expected to see the dog trailing behind like a shadow. Last summer he died so the gardener and his boy dug a pit in the shade of the big oak, cutting through turf and red earth until they hit the rough subsoil and jarred their spades.

They lined the grave with sacking and carefully lowered him in. The gentle old hound, curled up like a cat, neatly fitted the hole.

IV

Stiff purple-leaved basil and jasmine stars strung on a thread and draped, in early morning, over the glimmering icon.
Stoop to Mary, kiss cool glass, smell the garden.

V

She couldn't forgive the trees, not even the great copper beech refreshed by new, pink foliage at the bottom of the garden.
She could only see that complicit branch, the drop below, how he'd hung there.

VI

I hack back overgrown roses to gain access to the back of the house. Through the window I glimpse books stacked on the floor.
She lies in the chapel now. I saw her laid out, the coffin lid leaned beside – a doorway leading through the whitewashed wall.
Tucked in a shrub, a nest, small and round and empty. From the hawthorn by the cow field, bird song.

VII

Many generations lived together within the walled compound: children, parents, grandparents and the ancestors. The family's modest bungalow opened out into the garden by way of a wooden balcony and an area for cooking covered by rough thatch. Several narrow paths led off through lush vegetation – clumps of bamboo, palm fronds folded like fans, lime-green hostas. Here and there colour broke through the luxuriant foliage; magenta bougainvillea swept over a gateway, yellow-eyed lotuses stared out from the pond. Down one of the winding paths a wide bowl stood on a plinth. It was kept brimming with fresh water, frangipani blossom floated there. Beside the bowl the spirit house for the family's ancestors sheltered by a reed canopy. At night tea lights and a stone lantern glimmered on the altar table. By day exquisitely arranged fruit, titbits from a meal and garlands of flowers were brought, offerings that nurtured the links between those living in the garden and those who once washed rice and chatted there. The compound's walls were porous, eliding past and present, allowing the incarnated to mingle, speak and share food with spirits of the dead.

The grandmother, wasted and thin as an old cat, spent more and more of her time at the ancestors' shrine: talking to familiar spirits, praying or sitting in silence as moths fluttered around the lantern. She burned spirals of incense, sprinkled flower petals, steadily moving towards her future. Soon she would join the great tribe, that invisible gathering of well-wishers and string-pullers who wove their web over the garden.

VIII

Next morning the rescued nestling was dead. They'd fed it mashed egg yolk, touching the corner of its beak with a matchstick to coax it to open. Now the girl took it back to the garden to bury. All the previous day's wonder, when she'd felt the bird revive in her hand, was crushed. Putting the body into the ground struck the girl to the heart, like a betrayal. She wanted the chick to grow feathers and soar free. She hated how its slack skin hung from its cold, bulbous body.

After that, she trusted nothing. Plants, birds, people – under their colour and movement she always saw the failure of the resurrection.

IX

Under my father's apple tree peonies grew, forcing their way between the roots. Cool, crisp globes poised over a welter of new leaves, slowly fattening until the bud scales split, exposing seams of claret. The next day layers of petals spilled out like crinkled petticoats.
The peonies I now tend hang loose and floppy, softened by summer rain; petals bleached a tender pink, etched white at the edges. Gradually they slacken their tenuous hold, longing to fall.
Tomorrow the stalks, unfrocked, will bear naked seed heads, lumpy, unfamiliar forms that the sun will dry and curl. Then there'll be the letting go; the pod emptied and its answering – plenitude – seeds dispersed and flying on the wind.

X

In summer the cat chewed grass, flattened the catnip or lolled about on the baked earth beside the fence, her fur going matt from the dust. When the temperature rose, she slunk off to the fuchsia hedge or padded away to the fernery where she tormented loose-skinned frogs with the side of her paw. She drank from the stone bird bath, up on her back legs, not minding clouds of red algae and cherry stones. Once she sprang from the cover of a hydrangea, leaping four feet high to snatch a goldfinch out of the air. Now her bones turn brittle, drying to meal, nourishment for the weeping cherry's roots.

XI

Great cages of sharp-toothed brambles, long briars that shoot out, loop down and root in. They seize back the garden, re-capture the land I laboured to reclaim, where I, with such hope, once planned to grow you sweet peas and sunflowers.

XII

How can I alone cut down the sumac tree that grew so fast and then died suddenly this spring? Who now will dare perch with shears on the high beech hedge to bring it low? Whose whistling will I hear among the lupins?
Who will stand among the ferns, cigarette in one hand, hose pipe in the other? Who will cut the grass, put damp boots before the heat in winter? Who will hack roots, drag branches, rip hanks of ivy from the wall? Who will sweep the yard with me, one with water, the other with a brush?
Who will share shade and tea with me? Who will sniff the roses? Who will sing in another tongue, full of longing and Italy? Who will praise rain, wind, sun, the acrid smoke of the fire? Who?

XIII

I'll walk out to see the garden as usual, wishing to be under the sky, the smell of fox sharp and strong, the wind chill and clear. It won't be evening – it would be too sad a time with the reddish glow in the stone walls. Nor the night – that's too lonely a time for dying. I'll go in the best part of the day, following the dawn. I'll potter out in welly boots and rest breathless at the gate, look up the track with its straggling hedges to the lane. Perhaps it'll be a pain in my chest that makes me stagger and wonder who'll feed the chickens.

The dog will come near as I lie on the grass, panting and biting at burrs in his paws. As the sounds in the garden fade – the crows flying over, the dew dripping from the bars of the gate - I'm glad that he lies warm at my side. The cold creeps in and I gaze at the sky, brilliant with wind and movement. I feel reluctant, afraid, but glad for the radiant beauty of one last morning in the garden.

Later some walkers find me and run to fetch my neighbour, the farmer, a good man. On the day of my funeral he'll come with his tractor to my gate as I asked. The men lift me, set my coffin on the trailer. He'll drive the steep track I've climbed so many mornings from my garden to the lane, for the last time under sky.

XIV

Sometimes you shuck a pea pod and find bold green peas in the crisp furrow. But others remain small, pale, barely formed, as if the light never filtered through to them. There are no whys or wherefores, some simply tire.

For seven months the baby fattened, curled in her pod, turning, as sleeping lovers do, lost in body and comfort, fingers splaying and tightening as she paddled her watery orbit. She was child seed, dormant potential. Then she slowed, softened, revolved one last, lingering turn and stopped.

XV

Always after a bad day she started up, complaining, saying she wanted to go back. She still didn't feel at home in England even after seven years. It was St John's night. In Lithuania everyone had a holiday but here she had to go to the warehouse and pack groceries all night. At home there'd be folk dancing in the square, drinking, everyone going to the forest. They always went to the forest.

He thought about it too, how the night trees reared up taller, suddenly unfamiliar, and the ferns no longer green but an un-nameable night colour. They took torches and bottles of Standard Russian. Laughing, drinking and searching for the flower of the fern. They looked all night but no one ever found it.

Margarita started up again. 'Why don't we go back? In England St John's night is nothing – no fires, no parties, no looking for fern flowers.'

He went out for a smoke on the balcony, leaned on the rail and looked down at the street. Ten thirty and still not quite dark. It was useless to argue, to repeat the reasons for staying, when she was like this, homesick. He looked at the jumble of pots – parsley, thyme, a window box with flowers because she'd wanted flowers, like the garden back home. Here they had a grow-bag for three tomato plants. She'd put a low strip of plastic mesh around it. The little fence made it like a real garden, she said.

'Hey, Margarita,' he called. She was crying again, shaking, bowed over on the sofa. 'Come out in the garden,' he called. She started wiping her eyes and stood up. 'It's not a proper garden,' she said, coming to the door. 'You work as a gardener but we've only got a balcony. At home we'd have uncle's dacha and good beetroot for borscht.'

He held up a flower pot. 'What is it?' she asked, blowing her nose and reluctantly stepping out. 'A fern,' he said. 'They grow by the old water tank on the shady side of one of the houses.' She put her hand out and fingered the fronds. 'Hey, Margarita, let me get a photo. We'll show them back home, you in England searching for the flower of the fern.'

XVI

Long ago in the garden, she had crouched, Wellingtons
stamping a line into her calves, and stared into the
pond's green eye, at a world she could encompass. The
compost heap behind her steamed, its sour breath
forming endless ghostly blooms while her fingers
drifted, exploring the glutinous water, scooping and
releasing strands of algae. She drew out her hands –
two glass-green gloves. They felt vivid, alive, and not
quite her own. All afternoon a luminescent charge
fizzed on her skin.

In the lab, thirty years on, that charge still fizzed as she
peered into the microscope. On her slide the marvellous
Euglena viridis, a single cell that confounded definition.
Animal? Vegetable? It fixed the sun's rays with its
scarlet eyespot, beat time with its long flagellum. She
imagined millions of them whirling like dervishes –
seas, lakes, oceans, all teeming with microscopic
dancers.

XVII

Next door to the bike store with its jumble of pedals
and spokes, his shed. Bean canes, cobwebs, plant pots
piled like washing up. In the wood-warmed air, he
planted out seeds and potted on, tamping compost in
seed trays with his palms, a finger to dib the holes. He
hung onions from nails, clustered trophies that dribbled
white, wiggly roots down the wall. He always crouched
on the steps to tie their rustling stems onto lengths of
string.

Sometimes, in August, he took my hand and led me
across the threshold into the jungle air to see the
morning glory that clambered at the window. Together
we parted the leafy curtain to count blue bugles and the
new buds and see how yesterday's blooms fell slack and
crumpled.

XVIII

Despite digging deep, flies began to gather in the heat, attracted by the scent of decay. For the rest of the summer nobody went near the grave. Though he was missed this had little to do with the loss of the dog. It was more the neat, brown square that was cut like a trap door out of the lawn.

Such a door once swallowed Persephone. A wiry hand shot out, snatched her by the ankle, and hauled her under. The door snapped shut behind.

Strange though it may seem, after months in the darkness, Persephone grew used to captivity. Underneath with her dark lover she learned of a slow, earthy alchemy. She witnessed the secretive stages of growth: the folded forms of stem and leaves emerging inside seeds, starch grains crystallising in knobbed roots, the spring bulbs waiting.

Each winter's end she heard the sounds of her return; seed coats split, root hairs scratched and sap roared relentlessly as the trees began sucking again. Gallons of water gushed through the root-ways, pulled up towards the red buds that thirsted on the twigs above. This was the moment of Persephone's return, blasted back to the garden through the trap door newly greened with turf.

XIX

Yesterday a blue tit in the shed hit itself on the window and then flew to the high shelf, panting with fear. The cat crouched on the floor, watching, confident she would have the final say. I stepped inside, put a hand where the bird cowered on the shelf. It screamed, jabbed at my palm as I carried it out. The bird paused a few seconds as I opened my palm, blinking. Where was the death blow?

Later, a baby shrew – the cat batted it here and there on the patio. I took the tiny creature from her, pearl-grey fur smooth as felt, one eye a bright black dot, the other squeezed closed. The back legs like bent wires already stiff, yet its delicate, tapered nose wrinkling as if it just smelt something good.

Leaving the Garden

He went down to the tree where, in autumn, he'd hung the leaf door. He recalled painstakingly pinning it together with thorns. Now it was January. The door had slowly become disembodied, the leaves leached of substance. Once their autumn colours blazed in the sunlight, now only a tracery of veins and fragments of leaf blade persisted. These remnants trembled in the wind like a length of ghostly winter lace, a delicate outline that framed space and absence.

The leaf door had granted him access to the garden of gardens, but in this season he could only look through it to the garden of remembrance that lay beyond the garden. Soon the wind would erase even this, sweeping it aside like a veil.

He leant on the garden wall to look at the gravestones, the mossy plaques and pots of shrivelled flowers. Not long until the sap stirred, that unstoppable green avalanche waited below. He imagined a surge of growth ripping through the wintery cemetery. Damp patches of bluebells sprang up; grasses burst out and waggled feathered heads. Then dandelions snapping out of buds; cow parsley cranking open lace umbrellas; foxglove spikes jostling pink bells with speckled throats. Drifts of golden pollen swirled along the aisles between the graves. It would soon smell sweet again, he thought, the scent of azaleas gusting in like honey.

Rebecca Hubbard grew up on the Kent coast and now lives in a small Hertfordshire village but her family roots are both Welsh and English. She combines being head gardener at a Camphill Community for adults with special needs with teaching creative writing. She studied art history at Sussex University and recently gained an MA in creative writing at Brunel University. Her poetry appears in magazines including *Acumen*, *Smiths Knoll*, *Poetry Nottingham*, *Weyfarers*, *Pennine Platform* and *Writing Women*. She worked for several years as a freelance journalist writing features on a wide range of subjects. Rebecca practises a silent meditation of the heart and sits with the Quakers.